Famous Women in History

SYBIL LUDINGTON
MESSENGER FOR INDEPENDENCE

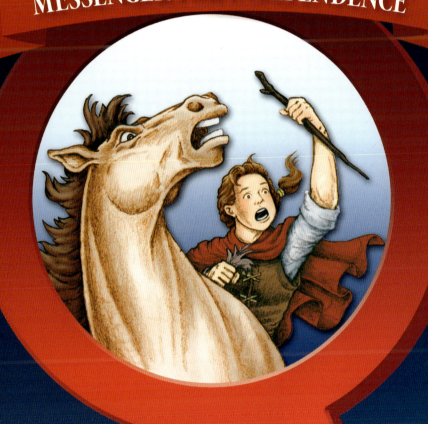

NICOLE K. ORR

© 2025 by Curious Fox Books™, an imprint of Fox Chapel Publishing Company, Inc.

Famous Women in History: Sybil Ludington is a revision of *Wonder Women: Heroines of History: Sybil Ludington*, published in 2019 by Purple Toad Publishing, Inc. Reproduction of its contents is strictly prohibited without written permission from the rights holder.

Paperback ISBN 979-8-89094-150-3
Hardcover ISBN 979-8-89094-151-0

Library of Congress Control Number: 2024947179

To learn more about the other great books from Fox Chapel Publishing, or to find a retailer near you, call toll-free 800-457-9112, send mail to , 903 Square Street, Mount Joy, PA 17552, or visit us at *www.FoxChapelPublishing.com*.

We are always looking for talented authors. To submit an idea, please send a brief inquiry to acquisitions@foxchapelpublishing.com.

Fox Chapel Publishing makes every effort to use environmentally friendly paper for printing.

Printed in China

CONTENTS

Chapter One
Old Enough to Be a Hero 4
Colonel Henry Ludington 9

Chapter Two
Teen Spirit 10
Enoch Crosby, Spy 17

Chapter Three
The Female Paul Revere 18
Paul Revere, Silversmith and Spy 23

Chapter Four
Whatever Happened to Sybil Ludington? 24
Why Was the Revolutionary War Important? 29

Chapter Five
Honoring Sybil Ludington 30
Having a Voice 39
Timeline 40
Chapter Notes 42
Further Reading 44
Books 44
Works Consulted 44
On the Internet 45
Glossary 46
Index 48

OLD ENOUGH TO BE A HERO

CHAPTER ONE

BANG! The door of Sybil Ludington's New York home was thrown open so fast, it slammed into the wall. She'd been sleeping a moment before, but now she was wide awake. Who would visit her family's farm so late at night, and why were they making so much noise? It was nearly 9:00 p.m., a strange time for a visitor.

"What is it?" Sybil's father asked as he headed for the disturbance. He stood tall and straight like the commander he was.

The newcomer did not speak. He was bent over with his hands on his knees. He was exhausted; his legs shook, and he smelled of sweat.

"Out with it, man!" Sybil's father, Colonel Henry Ludington, demanded. "What is the news from Danbury?" He kept his voice low, despite his urgent tone. Sybil's mother and her 11 siblings were still sound asleep.

Farms were great places to grow up for the most part. Once their chores were done, children could play outside. Children like Sybil often grew up with their first friends being their siblings and the animals on the farm. This was also where children learned many of their life skills, such as cooking and cleaning for girls or hunting and chopping firewood for boys.

CHAPTER ONE

Unlike many military men of his rank, Colonial Ludington was well liked by almost everybody who met him.

"They . . . they are attacking," the messenger gasped for air. "The British are already in Danbury. They are setting homes on fire. The people of Danbury need help!"

Oh, no! Danbury, Connecticut, was where the 7th Regiment of the Dutchess County Militia had moved all their food, tents, and clothing. Without those supplies, they would not be able to continue fighting. The men had just stashed these supplies and returned to their homes. The time for spring planting was near, and their families needed them.

"We must gather the militia," Colonel Henry said. "You!" He pointed at the messenger with intensity. "You must tell the Seventh of this attack. Tell them they must get to Danbury with utmost haste!"

"I cannot," said the man, as he finally straightened. Unlike Colonel Henry, his hands shook. "I have just come a very long way, and I do not know this area. If you send me, the Seventh may very well be too late to Danbury!"

Sybil's father looked at the messenger with frustration, then at the ceiling as if he were praying for patience. Then, he turned in Sybil's direction. In his eyes, she saw the same confidence he put in his men

Central Danbury as seen from atop Deer Hill in 1777. The building near the middle, with the tallest spire, is the Universalist Church. To the right of the church is the jail.

and the spies who regularly visited their home. He was putting that trust in her now.

"I know the area and I can ride hard," she said, her sleepiness forgotten. "Let me do this."

"You're young," he said.

"I'm sixteen." Sybil crossed her arms. "That'll have to be old enough."

A moment later, she was outside saddling her horse, Star. The animal knew the hills just as well as she did. There wasn't enough time for words between Sybil and her father. Instead, he handed her a stick. She nodded. Sybil knew how important her mission was. It seemed that

CHAPTER ONE

Panic forced many to take action when news of a British advance arrived. Here, General Philip Schuyler's wife, Catherine, sets fire to their wheat fields to keep them from the enemy. A messenger warns her of the British nearby. Later, the British burned down her house.

Star did, too. Together, they rode the fastest and hardest they'd ever gone.

"The British are burning Danbury. Muster at Ludington's at daybreak!"[1] She yelled the warning each time they rode by a farmhouse, slapping the doors with her stick. They rode from Carmel to Mahopac, from the Kent Cliffs to Farmers Mills. It rained endlessly, and it was so dark. She often heard strange noises, wondering if it was Skinners lingering about. Skinners were guerrilla fighters loyal to the British. Even though she was wary, she rode on.

When she returned home around dawn, she and Star were greeting with a wonderful sight. There were almost 400 men in the 7th Regiment of the Dutchess County Militia, and nearly all of them were mustered at the house.

"You were right." Her father waved her over. "Sixteen is old enough." No one knows for sure if this is how it happened exactly, but we do know for sure that it was an astonishing and brave accomplishment!

COLONEL HENRY LUDINGTON

Many things can be said of Colonel Henry Ludington, but no one can say he led a boring life. He was born in Branford, Connecticut, on May 25, 1739. He joined the military when he was 16 years old. At 21, he married Abigail. In the book titled *Sybil Ludington: The Call to Arms*, Henry Ludington is described as "above medium height, with blue eyes, he was a husky man with military bearing."[2] He spent so much of his life in service to his country, most people didn't use his name. They called him "The Colonel" instead.

During his career, Ludington worked with spies, served under kings, and for a while was a sub-sheriff. In 1776, he fought alongside General George Washington in the battle of White Plains, New York. At the time of Sybil's famous ride, Ludington was in charge of the 7th Regiment of the Dutchess County Militia. His regiment became so well known throughout New York, people simply called it "The Colonel's Regiment."[3]

Little is known of what became of Colonel Ludington after the war ended. All that historians know for sure is that he died in Putnam County, New York, on January 24, 1817.

The grist mill at the Ludington home.

TEEN SPIRIT

CHAPTER TWO

Sixteen years old, in the eyes of many cultures, is very young. In most of the United States, 16-year-olds are old enough to drive, but they cannot vote in elections, marry without a parent's permission, or join the military.

This was not the case in the mid-1700s. Sybil's father, Henry Ludington, joined the military at age 16. He spent most of his life serving his country. One of the most important things he did was in 1759. He led 60 Connecticut soldiers from Quebec, Canada, to Boston, Massachusetts. That was nearly 400 miles! Just before the journey, Ludington stopped to visit his uncle. He was there just long enough to meet his distant cousin, Abigail. Willis Fletcher Johnson's memoir of Colonel Ludington said this about that brief meeting: "[W]e may easily imagine the boy soldier's carrying with him into the northern wilderness an affectionate memory of his little

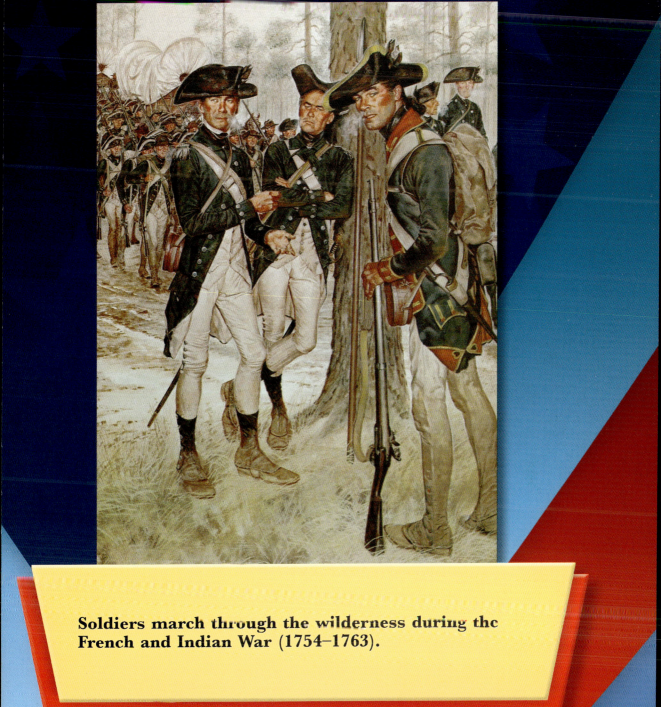

Soldiers march through the wilderness during the French and Indian War (1754–1763).

CHAPTER TWO

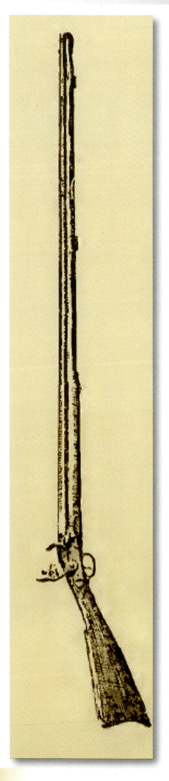

cousin, perhaps the last of his kin to bid him good-by, and also her cherishing a romantic regard for the lad whom she had seen march away with his comrades."1

The long trip was difficult. It was winter and most of the men in Ludington's care were wounded. When the journey was over, the 20-year-old went back to his uncle's home to see the girl he hadn't stopped thinking about. On May 1, 1760, Henry and Abigail were married. Within a year, they had their first child, a daughter named Sybil.

From the moment Sybil Ludington was born on April 5, 1761, she was surrounded by danger. The Revolutionary War was on the way. The British colonies in America wanted their freedom from Great Britain. As a child, Sybil wouldn't have much impact on her country's future. As a young adult, however, she would save her father's life and a whole city.

Just after she was born, Sybil and her parents moved to Dutchess County, New York. Over time, this area came to be called the Fredericksburg Precinct and then the town of Kent, in Putnam County. With almost 230 acres of land

A sketch of the rifle Colonel Ludington used during the French and Indian War. It was drawn by his great-great-granddaughter, Alice.

TEEN SPIRIT

Dutchess County, the place where a young Sybil Ludington would begin to make her mark in history.

surrounding her new home, there was much work for her parents to do and plenty of room for Sybil to play.

While Sybil grew up caring for her siblings and playing in the woods, the world around her grew more and more dangerous. Eight years of war were on the horizon. The signs of the coming revolution were everywhere. The fighting wasn't happening on the battlefield yet, but there were skirmishes in taverns, schoolhouses, and backyards. No one knew whom to trust. At the time, an accidental insult could easily spark outright violence.

The Ludington land was beautiful—and it was vital to the war effort. Messengers, the commanders of other regiments, and American spies regularly visited the Ludington home. One spy who often came to Sybil's house was Enoch Crosby. He trusted Sybil and her younger sister Rebecca to guard the house. He trusted them so much, he taught the

CHAPTER TWO

Enoch Crosby was one the few people who noticed Sybil's strength. He was impressed by her and valued her bravery.

girls secret signals. The sisters could use these with him and with each other if they thought the enemy was watching or listening.[2]

There was another reason the location of the Ludington house was so important. When the British attacked, the most direct route from Long Island, New York, to Connecticut was through the Ludingtons' land. Henry Ludington's orders were to assist nearby troops as needed, as well as to locate and reveal Tories (Americans loyal to the British). Ludington carried out his orders perfectly. He angered the British so much, a reward was offered to anyone who could bring him in dead or alive. One night sometime between 1776 and 1777, a man named Ichabod Prosser decided he wanted this reward. If it hadn't been for Sybil and Rebecca, Prosser might have succeeded.

By this time, Sybil had seven siblings. As the eldest, Sybil helped teach, protect, and raise her brothers and sisters. When Prosser and his men arrived, she planned a trick. Sybil and Rebecca quietly went into the house and told the rest of their family. Immediately, candles were lit in every window. As Prosser and his men watched, figures marched back and forth inside the home. Historian Louis S. Patrick later described the scene: "These fearless girls, with guns in hand, were acting as sentinels, pacing the piazza to and fro in true military style and grit to guard their father against surprise."[3] Prosser was certain that the building was full of soldiers. When daybreak came, he gave up and rode away with his men. They had no idea that the figures they had seen marching had not been soldiers. They had been children bravely pretending.

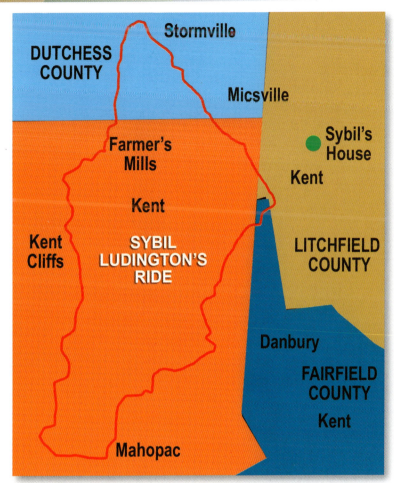

The red line shows the route Sybil took on her famous ride.

CHAPTER TWO

This statue by Anna Huntington was the first one made of Sybil Ludington. Most of the statues that followed were based on this one.

Of Henry Ludington's survival, Louis S. Patrick later said, "The Colonel's most vigilant and watchful companion was his sentinel daughter, Sibbell [sic]." This event was the first time history saw how important Sybil Ludington was.[4]

ENOCH CROSBY, SPY

In 1821, author James Fenimore Cooper released a book titled *The Spy: A Tale of the Neutral Ground*. The story introduced spy Harvey Birch, and it was thrilling. It showed the Revolutionary War in more detail than people had seen before. Readers wanted to know who Cooper's sources were. Had Cooper based his hero on a real person? Eventually it was discovered that the character Harvey Birch had been loosely based on a real spy named Enoch Crosby. Then, on October 15, 1832, Crosby went to the Putnam County Court with the real story.

Born in Massachusetts on January 4, 1750, Crosby began as a shoemaker. At age 16, he joined the military, but not as a regular soldier. Beginning in 1776, he worked for the New York State Committee and Commission for Detecting and Defeating Conspiracies. This group, under John Jay, was the country's first spy agency. Crosby was a double agent. Depending on who caught him in his travels, Crosby would change which side he was on. This gave him the ability to gather information other men couldn't. Not even Crosby's family knew what he was working on for the Patriots.

During his six years as a double agent, Crosby was often arrested by soldiers on both sides of the war and put through fake trials. One of the few places he could sleep safely was the Ludington house.

Crosby's missions were dangerous, but to him, they were worth it. Toward the end of his life, he wrote, "Having been spared to enjoy these blessings—independence and prosperity—for half a century and see them still continued, I can lay down my weary and worn out limbs in peace and happiness."[5]

THE FEMALE PAUL REVERE

CHAPTER THREE

If Sybil Ludington's ride in 1777 was so important to the Revolutionary War, why didn't her story make it into history books until many years after her death? Why aren't there more statues of her, more movies about her life, or more stories of her childhood?

Sybil Ludington's role in the battle for Danbury was never celebrated because she was a woman. During her lifetime, women were rarely involved in wars. Most often, they nursed the wounded or repaired damaged uniforms. While her father and her father's regiment appreciated Sybil's ride, it was largely ignored by history.

There are many names that come to mind when people talk about the Revolutionary War. Joseph Warren helped lead and organize the Patriots. Warren employed Paul Revere, a silversmith who worked as a messenger. Revere carried warnings, updates, and orders to people when the information couldn't be trusted to the postal service. On April 18, 1775, Revere delivered a message just like Sybil Ludington

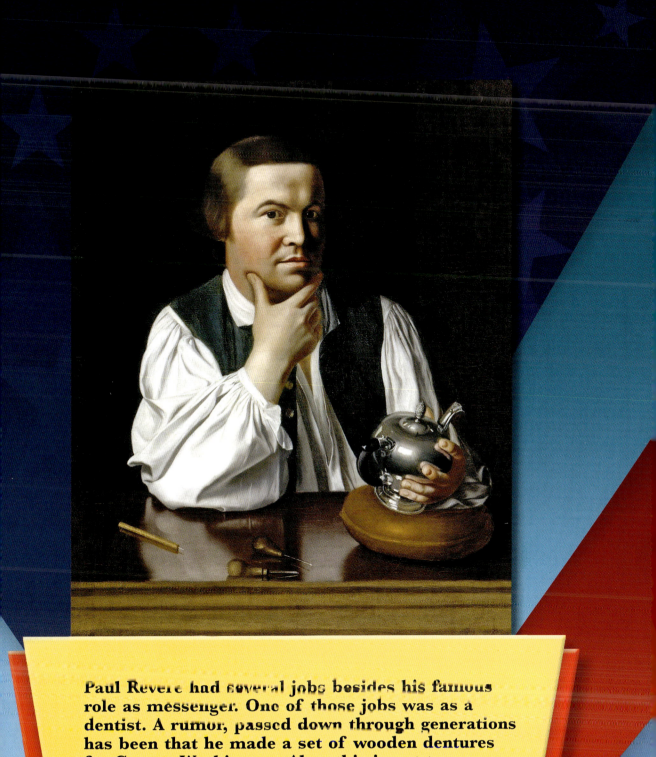

Paul Revere had several jobs besides his famous role as messenger. One of those jobs was as a dentist. A rumor, passed down through generations has been that he made a set of wooden dentures for George Washington. Alas, this is not true.

CHAPTER THREE

did. Joseph Warren had told Revere to ride from Boston to Concord, Massachusetts. Just as with Danbury, Connecticut, Concord was where the local militia stored their guns, powder, and ammunition. Warning had already been sent to Concord for them to hide everything important in barns, wells, and even swamps. Now Revere needed to take them a different, more important warning. The British were coming for Concord, but they weren't coming by land like everyone thought. They were coming by water. Revere needed to alert the militia, and he had to reach Concord before the British.[1]

While Sybil made her trip entirely by horse, Revere began by boat. His mission almost ended there. As he and a few other men were preparing to cross the Charles River, Revere realized he had forgotten the cloth rags to wrap the oars. Without them, the oars would splash loud enough to give them all away. According to legend, a woman was there, wearing a petticoat. She gave the undergarment to the men, who ripped it into pieces and used them to wrap the oars. Considering the times, it would have been highly unusual for a woman to hand over her petticoat.[2]

Once across the Charles River, Revere continued on horseback. He could have gone directly to Concord, but he made an important stop in Lexington, Massachusetts. Revere actually had two missions. This other mission was to warn two patriot leaders staying in

Paul Revere prepares to row across the Charles River toward Concord. Any loud noises would have alerted the British.

20

THE FEMALE PAUL REVERE

Lexington. Their names were Samuel Adams and John Hancock—and the British planned to arrest them both. If the British succeeded, the war might tip in their favor.

Revere arrived in Lexington and delivered his warning to Adams and Hancock. He then met up with the other messenger Warren had dispatched, William Dawes. Once joined by a third man, Dr. Samuel Prescott, the group set out for Concord. They were attacked before they got there. Revere was captured, but the other two messengers rode on.

Revere wasn't held for long. When he was released, he didn't try to catch up with Dawes and Prescott. Instead, he went back to Lexington and helped Adams and Hancock escape the British.

The silversmith called Revere, who made items ranging from sword hilts to a chain for a pet squirrel, would make his ride matter at all cost.

Sybil Ludington and Paul Revere had a lot in common. They both served as messengers. Sybil rode through the countryside, telling the men that the British were coming to Danbury. Revere rode toward Concord to tell them the British were coming for the ammunition kept there. This, however, is where the similarities end. Sybil succeeded in delivering her message. Revere was caught, forcing Dr. Samuel Prescott and William Dawes to ride on without him. Sybil rode 40 miles in one

21

CHAPTER THREE

Revere rode back to Lexington to help Adams and Hancock escape.

night. Revere rode only half that before being taken by the British. Sybil was known to have said, "The British are burning Danbury. Muster at Ludington's at daybreak!"[3] History reports that Revere shouted, "The British are coming!" This is very unlikely. Revere, and the men traveling with him, were passing through dangerous areas full of the enemy. Shouting would have gotten them all captured or killed.

In the same way that Paul Revere's story has been muddled by history, so has Sybil Ludington's story become unclear. Historians know what day and time she rode into the night, but no one can agree who sent her. Did her father ask her to go? Did Sybil volunteer? No one has the answers. Some sources say Sybil was attacked during her ride. They say she had to use her stick to defend herself against Skinners and Redcoats.

Sybil Ludington received very little thanks during her lifetime. The only acknowledgments were from the 7th Regiment, the people of Danbury, and General Washington. For Sybil, who had risked her life twice for her father and the war, that was thanks enough.

PAUL REVERE, SILVERSMITH AND SPY

Paul Revere is best known for his famous ride, but he was more than a messenger during the war. Born on January 1, 1735, in Boston, Massachusetts, he was a family man from the beginning of his life to the end. He grew up with seven siblings. As an adult, he married twice and had 16 children. He loved his kids so deeply, he often called them his "little lambs."4 Incredibly, he was a grandfather to at least 51 children.

When he was a teenager, Revere was a bell ringer. Starting around the age of 15, he began going to the Eight Bell Church near his house to ring the bells. Soon he started to bring a few friends. Together, they created bell-ringing team. Membership was difficult to get and the rules were strict. This likely taught Revere the leadership skills he would later need for the military.

One of Revere's first jobs was as a silversmith, a trade he learned from his father. By the time he died at age 83 in 1818, Revere had made more than 900 church bells. He also made printing plates, which were used to print money. Revere also created some controversial pieces. After a riot between Patriots and British soldiers in which five civilians were killed, Revere created artwork that called the event the Boston Massacre. The name stuck. In 1771, he set up reminders in the windows of his home, showing three different scenes from that day.

Revere was also part of a spy ring. Created around 1774, the spy ring was called both the Mechanics and the Liberty Boys. They reported to the leaders of the Sons of Liberty.

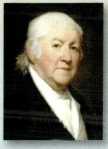

Paul Revere at 78

WHATEVER HAPPENED TO SYBIL LUDINGTON?

CHAPTER FOUR

Sybil's 40-mile-ride did not save Danbury from destruction. The British still burned the city to the ground. They still consumed or scattered the supplies that were kept there. What Sybil's warning did accomplish was saving Danbury itself. If the 7th Regiment had not chased the British away, the Redcoats could have stayed in the city and made it their own. Instead, Colonel Ludington and his 400 men flooded into Danbury and drove the Redcoats out. Next, Ludington marched his regiment another 17 miles to Ridgefield, Connecticut. There, they beat the British back in one of the most important victories of the war.

Other battles would follow. Colonel Ludington would spend most of his life serving his country. His daughter's role in the war, however, was over. While she was a messenger a few more times, none of those rides was as dangerous as her first. At the end of the war, Sybil had the chance to lead a normal life.

Sybil fearlessly rode from home to home, warning families of the incoming danger. She gave the people precious time to gather what they needed and get to safety.

CHAPTER FOUR

As the daughter of Colonel Henry Ludington, Sybil Ludington had led an exciting life. In Catskill, New York, she was finally able to live quietly and happily for a while.

On October 24, 1784, 23-year-old Sybil married Edmond Ogden. The two of them moved to Catskill, New York. The couple only had one son, whom they named Henry after Sybil's father. Gone were the days of watching for enemy soldiers through the windows. Sybil did not want to give her son the same dangerous childhood she had had. Instead, the family of three could spend the rest of their lives away from war, regiments, and late-night messages.[1]

For a very long time, historians were unable to agree on what happened to Sybil Ludington after her son was born. So much of the information they had was from unreliable sources. Plaques, statues, articles—all of them seemed to contradict one another. Did Sybil and

WHATEVER HAPPENED TO SYBIL LUDINGTON?

her husband have one child named Henry? Was it possible they had four boys and two girls? Had her husband's name been Edmond or Henry? Did the couple meet as adults or had they known each other since they were children? Did the two run a tavern together, or did Sybil buy her own tavern? Did Edmond die when his son was barely a teenager, or did Sybil die first? These questions and more haunted historians for years. It wasn't until the year 2000 that the answers finally came to light. The answers were in the book *Sybil Ludington: The Call to Arms*, by Vincent Dacquino, published that year.

In 1799, Sybil's husband died of yellow fever. Henry was only 13 years old, and Sybil would have to raise him alone. In 1803, she bought a tavern and ran it for many years. Just like delivering messages during the American Revolution, being a tavern keeper was not considered appropriate work for a woman in New York. "She became a model for all single mothers," Dacquino said in an interview with *The Newtown Bee*.[2] In a time when women were limited in their job options, Sybil constantly took risks and ignored the judgment of others. She originally bought her tavern for $732. Six years later, she sold it for nearly $3,000.[3]

Henry Ogden became a lawyer and joined the military. In 1810, he married Julia Peck. The next year, they gave Sybil a grandson named Edmund Augustus.

The family was very close. When Henry and his family moved to Unadilla, New York, they took Sybil with them. There, she spent the next nine years—the last years of her life. In 1838, she asked the military for the pension they owed her because of her marriage to Edmond Ogden. Unfortunately, since she could not find her marriage certificate, the military refused her request. When Sybil died a year later, on February 26, 1839, she did not have a lot of money. She was, however, surrounded by family.

CHAPTER FOUR

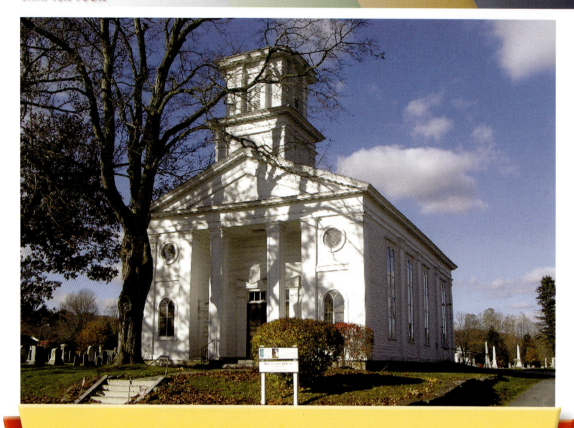

Sybil Ludington was laid to rest in Maple Avenue Cemetery, adjacent to Patterson Church (above), which is also where her father was buried.

Sybil played several roles during her lifetime. As a child, she was a guard, a messenger, and a protector of spies. As an adult, she was a wife, a tavern keeper, a mother, and a grandmother. All these years later, Sybil remains a symbol of strength and courage.

WHY WAS THE REVOLUTIONARY WAR IMPORTANT?

The Revolutionary War was also called the War for Independence. Before the United States existed, Great Britain controlled its Thirteen American Colonies. As the colonies became more populated, Great Britain continued to pass new laws and taxes—without any votes from the colonists.

The colonists began to protest. They argued that they should have a voice in matters that affected them. In 1774, they became frustrated enough to form their own government. Its first meeting was called the Continental Congress. By the time they held the Second Continental Congress, the colonists were ready to announce that they would no longer be controlled by Great Britain. They did not want to be ruled by a far-off king. They wanted to be ruled by the people who lived in the colonies. When the first shot of the eight-year-war was fired on April 19, 1775, it was called the "shot heard round the world."

The line "The shot heard round the world" was made famous by the poem "Concord Hymn," by Ralph Waldo Emerson.

HONORING SYBIL LUDINGTON

CHAPTER FIVE

What do a U.S. postage stamp, a marathon in New York, and a holiday celebrated each year on April 26 have in common? These are just three of the many ways Sybil Ludington is now honored for her contribution to the Revolutionary War.

When Sybil Ludington died in 1839, it seemed her name died with her. Then, around 1880, Martha J. Lamb wrote a book on the history of New York called *History of the City of New York: Its Origin, Rise, and Progress*. Most of Lamb's research was done by exchanging letters with descendants of the Ludington family. Sybil was barely mentioned, but Lamb described her as a "spirited young girl of sixteen."[1]

In 1907, more of Sybil's story began to unfold. Willis Fletcher Johnson wrote a book titled *Colonel Henry Ludington: A Memoir*. Of Sybil's ride, he said, "[S]

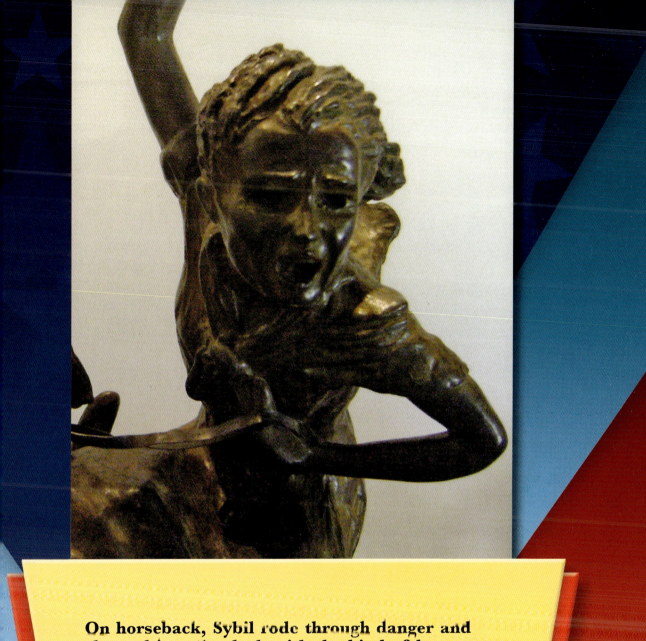

On horseback, Sybil rode through danger and shouted into the dark with the kind of bravery many women have mustered throughout history.

CHAPTER FIVE

The DAR has been involved in maintaining the legacies of many historical figures. Sybil Ludington is just one example. Betsy Ross, the woman said to have designed the first American flag, is another.

he performed her task, clinging to a man's saddle, and guiding her steed . . . as she rode through the night."[2]

One of the first organizations to get excited about Sybil's ride was the Daughters of the American Revolution (DAR). All members of DAR are female and descended from a person or family who was vital to America's fight for independence. In 1935, members of the Enoch Crosby Chapter of DAR, as well as a few other organizations, came together to place markers along the route Sybil rode. This was done to honor Sybil's risky journey and to show the rest of the world how amazing the teenager's accomplishment actually was. For DAR, Sybil

HONORING SYBIL LUDINGTON

quickly came to symbolize independence, strength, and female bravery. This message grew so important to DAR, they put up one of the first statues of Sybil at DAR's headquarters in Washington, D.C.

There are several other statues of this famous teenager. One of them is outside the library in Danbury. Almost all of these are copies based on the first statue, which sits in Carmel, New York. It was built by Anna Hyatt Huntington and was finished in 1961. The statue shows Sybil's horse Star with its head held high. Sybil rides sidesaddle as she holds

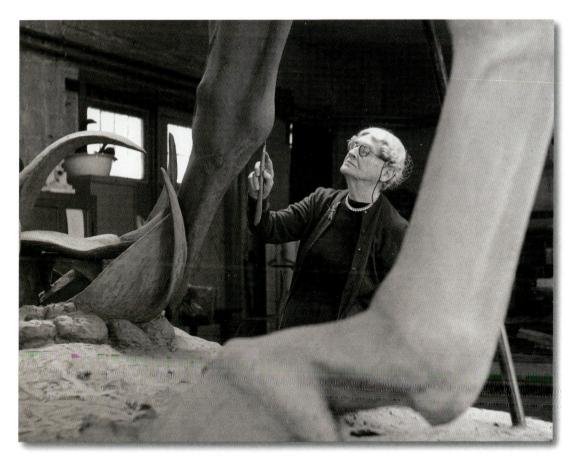

Anna Hyatt Huntington was one of the first female sculptors in the United States. She created the first public monument by a woman in New York City in 1915.

CHAPTER FIVE

Contributors to the Cause was a series of stamps hosted by the post office. In addition to Ludington, there was also a stamp of Harriet Tubman.

her stick high above her head. Her expression is intense, her eyes serious. In 1975, the U.S. Postal Service printed an 8-cent stamp with Sybil Ludington on it. This was part of the "Contributors to the Cause" stamp series. Just as with her statues, Sybil is shown on horseback, waving her stick over her head. On the stamp, Danbury burns in the background.

As the route Sybil took grew more and more interesting to the world, an event was created so that people could experience her ride firsthand. The tradition began in 1979 as a marathon run of nearly 31 miles. It started and ended in Carmel, New York, near the original statue of Sybil.

The people of Carmel grew so proud of the Sybil story, some of them consider the yearly anniversary of Sybil's ride a holiday. Each year on April 26, people visit Sybil's grave in Patterson, New York. They also write 1777 on their hands. Much of the world might not recognize the date, but in New York, the number stands for teenage independence.

As the years continued to speed by, Sybil's story grew and grew. She was nicknamed the Female Paul Revere. The world wanted to know as much about her as possible. At the Putnam County Golf Course, Sybil's image was printed on golf balls. There was a musical about her called

HONORING SYBIL LUDINGTON

Heroine on Horseback: The Ballad of Sybil Ludington. In 1993, an opera was produced called *Sybil: Daughter of the American Revolution*. In 2010, the film *Sybil Ludington: The Female Paul Revere* was released. The board game *Ludington's Ride* lets players follow Sybil's exact route on a map.

Statues of Sybil Ludington have been erected outside of New England. This one is at the Offner Sculpture Learning and Research Center near Myrtle Beach, South Carolina.

CHAPTER FIVE

For the longest time, Paul Revere's reputation still outdid Sybil's. Much of this was because of a poem written by Henry Wadsworth Longfellow. It begins:

> Listen, my children, and you shall hear
> Of the midnight ride of Paul Revere,
> On the eighteenth of April, in Seventy-Five:
> Hardly a man is now alive
> Who remembers that famous day and year.[3]

Sybil, however, has begun to catch up. There are at least two poems written about her. One of them, inspired by Longfellow, was written by Berton Braley in 1940. It begins like this:

> Listen, my children, and you shall hear
> Of a lovely feminine Paul Revere
> Who rode an equally famous ride
> Through a different part of the countryside,
> Where Sybil Ludington's name recalls
> A ride as daring as that of Paul's.[4]

In the years since Sybil's death, and since her story has become clearer, her name has come to mean many things. *Strong* and *heroic* are just two of them. Historian Paula Hunt probably summed up Sybil the best when she wrote: "In the end, Sybil Ludington has embodied the possibilities—courage, individuality, loyalty—that Americans of different genders, generations, and political persuasions have considered to be the highest aspirations for themselves and for their country. The story

The courage of Sybil Ludington will continue to be displayed through the many statues and paintings of her for years to come.

CHAPTER FIVE

of the lone, teenage girl riding for freedom, it seems, is simply too good not to be believed."[5]

Sybil Ludington did something else too. Because of the dangerous ride she took, she proved that it doesn't matter if people say you're too young or not as strong as someone else. Because of her midnight ride, Sybil Ludington showed young women everywhere that they already have everything they need to change the world.

Sybil Ludington is buried near the Patterson Church, alongside her father and her mother.

38

HAVING A VOICE

When the Daughters of the American Revolution was formed in 1890, women had little voice. In most parts of the country, they weren't allowed to vote, be members of the government, or join the military. The Revolutionary War was long over, but the desire for female independence was still strong. DAR was formed with three objectives:

1. Historical, including protecting historic sites, finding the forgotten graves of war heroes, and marking locations where important events happened.
2. Educational, including teaching the youth of today how important freedom and independence are and about the people who have fought for these ideals.
3. Patriotic, including mailing care packages to soldiers overseas, giving out patriotic awards, and helping care for veterans.

DAR's message has grown more popular over the years. With more than 950,000 women joining since its creation, DAR is just one of the ways that women are gaining strength and influence.[6]

Statue in front of DAR headquarters

TIMELINE

1761   Sybil Ludington is born on April 5 in Kent, New York.

1775   The morning after Paul Revere's Midnight Ride, the Revolutionary War begins.

1777   Sybil rides into the night to gather the 7th Regiment of the Dutchess County Militia.

1783   The Revolutionary War ends with the surrender of Great Britain.

1784   Sybil marries Edmond Ogden; they move to Catskill, New York.

1786   Sybil and Edmond have a son named Henry Ogden.

1799   Edmond Ogden dies of yellow fever.

1803   Sybil buys a tavern. She will sell it at a profit six years later.

1811   Edmund Augustus, Sybil's first grandson, is born.

1839   Sybil dies on February 26.

1935   The Daughters of the American Revolution and other organizations work together to place markers along the path Sybil Ludington rode.

1961   A statue of Sybil is placed at Lake Gleneida in Carmel, New York.

1975   A stamp of Sybil is made as part of the U.S. Postal Service's Contributors to the Cause series.

1993   The opera *Sybil: Daughter of the American Revolution* premieres.

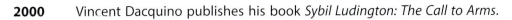

TIMELINE

2000   Vincent Dacquino publishes his book *Sybil Ludington: The Call to Arms*.

2002   PBS Kids airs a *Liberty's Kids* episode on Sybil Ludington.

2010   A movie of Sybil's ride titled *Sybil Ludington: The Female Paul Revere* is released.

2018   Work begins on a board game called *Ludington's Ride*.

CHAPTER NOTES

Chapter One. Old Enough to Be a Hero
1. History of American Women. "New York Heroine of the Revolutionary War." August 2010. https://www.womenhistoryblog.com/2010/08/sybil-ludington.html
2. Dacquino, Vincent. *Sybil Ludington: The Call to Arms*. Fleischmanns, NY: Purple Mountain Press, 2000.
3. Ibid.

Chapter Two: Teen Spirit
1. Johnson, Willis Fletcher. *Colonel Henry Ludington: A Memoir*. New York: Printed by His Grandchildren Lavinia Elizabeth Ludington and Charles Henry Ludington, 1907, pp. 35–36. Available at https://www.loc.gov/resource/gdcmassbookdig.colonelhenryludi00john/?sp=55&st=image
2. Ibid.
3. Patrick, Louis S. "Secret Service of the American Revolution." The Connecticut Society of the Sons of the American Revolution. Reprinted from *The Connecticut Magazine*, 1907. https://www.sarconnecticut.org/secret-service-of-the-american-revolution/
4. Ibid.
5. Levine, David. "How a Shoemaker Turned into a Spy." *Hudson Valley Magazine*. May 28, 2014. https://hvmag.com/uncategorized/how-a-shoemaker-turned-into-a-spy/

Chapter Three: The Female Paul Revere
1. "Paul Revere's Midnight Ride." United States History. Not dated. https://www.u-s-history.com/pages/h1261.html
2. Ibid.
3. "New York Heroine of the Revolutionary War." *History of American Women*. August 2010. https://www.womenhistoryblog.com/2010/08/sybil-ludington.html
4. "11 Things You Probably Didn't Know About Paul Revere." *Mental Floss*. January 16, 2015. https://www.mentalfloss.com/article/60915/11-things-you-probably-didnt-know-about-paul-revere

CHAPTER NOTES

Chapter Four. Whatever Happened to Sybil Ludington?
1. Howard, Jan. "Uncovering the Remarkable Story of Sybil Ludington." *The Newtown [Connecticut] Bee*. April 11, 2001. https://www.newtownbee.com/04112001/uncovering-the-remarkable-story-of-sybil-ludington/
2. Ibid.
3. Ibid.

Chapter Five. Honoring Sybil Ludington
1. "Sybil Ludington Statue." *The Clio*. April 27, 2017. https://theclio.com/entry/38254
2. Johnson, Willis Fletcher. *Colonel Henry Ludington: A Memoir*. New York: Printed by His Grandchildren Lavinia Elizabeth Ludington and Charles Henry Ludington, 1907, p. 90. Available at https://www.loc.gov/resource/gdcmassbookdig.colonelhenryludi00john/?sp=55&st=image
3. Longfellow, Henry Wadsworth. *Paul Revere's Ride*. Poets.org. https://poets.org/poem/paul-reveres-ride
4. "New York Heroine of the Revolutionary War." *History of American Women*. August 2010. https://www.womenhistoryblog.com/2010/08/sybil-ludington.html
5. Hunt, Paula D. "Sybil Ludington, the Female Paul Revere: The Making of a Revolutionary War Heroine." *New England Quarterly*, Vol. 88, no. 2, June 2015: pp. 221–222. https://www.mitpressjournals.org/doi/pdf/10.1162/TNEQ_a_00452
6. Daughters of the American Revolution. "What We Do." https://www.dar.org/national-society/what-we-do

FURTHER READING

Books

Abbott, E. F. *Sybil Ludington: Revolutionary War Rider*. New York: Square Fish Publishing, 2014.

Amstel, Marsha, and Ted Hammond. *The Horse-Riding Adventure of Sybil Ludington, Revolutionary War Messenger*. Minneapolis: Graphic Universe, 2011.

Casey, Susan. *Women Heroes of the American Revolution: 20 Stories of Espionage, Sabotage, Defiance, and Rescue*. Chicago: Chicago Review Press, 2017.

Edwards, Roberta. *Who Was Paul Revere?* New York: Penguin Workshop, 2011.

Longfellow, Henry Wadsworth. *Paul Revere's Ride*. New York: Applesauce Press, 2014.

Mara, Wil. *Paul Revere: American Freedom Fighter*. New York: Children's Press, 2015.

Marsico, Katie. *Sybil Ludington's Revolutionary War Story*. Minneapolis: Lerner Classroom, 2018.

Works Consulted

Cohen, Jennie. "10 Things You May Not Know About Paul Revere." *History*, April 16, 2013. Updated August 9, 2023. https://www.history.com/news/11-things-you-may-not-know-about-paul-revere

Dacquino, Vincent. *Sybil Ludington: The Call to Arms*. Fleischmanns, NY: Purple Mountain Press, 2000.

DeBenedette, Valerie. "Sybil Ludington: The 16-Year-Old Revolutionary Who Outrode Paul Revere." *Mental Floss*. April 18, 2020. https://www.mentalfloss.com/article/78686/16-year-old-revolutionary-who-outrode-paul-revere

FURTHER READING

Fisher, Nicole. "Meet Revolutionary Woman Sybil Ludington Ogden." The Federalist, March 30, 2016. https://thefederalist.com/2016/03/30/meet-revolutionary-woman-sybil-ludington-ogden/

Johnson, Willis Fletcher. *Colonel Henry Ludington: A Memoir*. New York: Lavinia Elizabeth Ludington and Charles Henry Ludington, 1907. Available at https://www.loc.gov/resource/gdcmassbookdig.colonelhenryludi00john/?sp=55&st=image

Lewis, Jone Johnson. "Sybil Ludington: A Female Paul Revere?" *Thought Co.*, July 31, 2017. https://www.thoughtco.com/sybil-ludington-biography-3530671

National Women's History Museum: "Sybil Ludington." https://www.nwhm.org/education-resources/biographies/sybil-ludington

Patrick, Louis S. "Secret Service of the American Revolution." *Connecticut Star*, 1907.

On the Internet

"Sybil Ludington." *Greatest Stories Ever Told*. RevolutionaryWar.net. https://www.revolutionary-war.net/sybil-ludington.html

"Sybil Ludington, the Teen Patriot Who Outrode Paul Revere." *Kids Discover*, April 8, 2015. https://www.kidsdiscover.com/quick-reads/sybil-ludington-teen-patriot-outrode-paul-revere/

GLOSSARY

aspiration (as-pur-AY-shun)—A high goal.

comrade (KAHM-rad)—A fellow soldier.

conspiracy (kon-SPEER-uh-see)—A secret plot organized by a group of people to do something illegal.

contribution (kon-trih-BYOO-shun)—An important part or role in a larger action; a gift or payment.

guerrilla (guh-RIL-uh)—A person who fights for a unit that is independent of the major forces in a war.

kin—Family.

marathon (MAYR-uh-thon)—A long-distance footrace.

muddle (MUH-dul)—To make unclear; mix together; confuse.

Patriot (PAY-tree-it)—One who loves his or her country; during the Revolutionary War, a soldier fighting for independence.

pension (PEN-shun)—Money paid following retirement or to the surviving dependents.

piazza (pee-AH-zah)—A porch or open area.

Redcoat (RED-koht)—A British soldier in the regular army.

sentinel (SEN-tih-nul)—A person who stands watch.

GLOSSARY

A farm in New England in the 1700s

side saddle (SYD SAD-ul)—Sitting with both legs to one side of the saddle.

Skinner (SKIH-ner)—Any of the American soldiers trained by Cortlandt Skinner, a general from New Jersey who fought for the British.

vigilant (VIH-jih-lent)—Keeping careful watch for danger.

PHOTO CREDITS: Cover, p 1—J. Rasemas; pp. 2–3—Burke & Atwell, Chicago; p. 5—Benson Lossing LOC; pp. 6, 8, 9, 11, 12, 14, 17 (background), 22, 23, 26, 29 (background), 33, 34 34, 39 (background)—Public Domain; p. 7—Pictures Now/ Alamy Stock Photo; p. 13—Doug Kerr; pp. 16, 28, 38—Anthony22; p. 19—J.S. Copley; p. 20—Boston Public Library p. 21—Internet Archive Book Images; pp. 25, 41—Iconspng; p. 29—National Guard; p.p. 31, 35—Doug Coldwell; p. 32—Aude; p. 37—RVC845; p. 39—AgnostocPreachersKid. Every measure has been taken to find all copyright holders of material used in this book. In the event any mistakes or omissions have happened within, attempts to correct them will be made in future editions of the book.

47

INDEX

Adams, Samuel 21, 22
Augustus, Edmund (grandson) 27
Braley, Berton 36
Colonel Henry Ludington: A Memoir 30
Contributors to the Cause 34
Cooper, James Fenimore 17
Crosby, Enoch 13, 14, 17, 32
Dacquino, Vincent 27
Daughters of the American Revolution (DAR) 32–33, 39
Dawes, William 21
Hancock, John 21, 22
Heroine on Horseback: the Ballad of Sybil Ludington 35
History of the City of New York: Its Origin, Rise, and Progress 30
Huntington, Anna Hyatt 16, 33
Hunt, Paula 36
Jay, John 17
Johnson, Willis Fletcher 10, 12, 30, 32
Lamb, Martha J. 30
Liberty Boys 23
Longfellow, Henry Wadsworth 36
Ludington, Abigail (mother) 9, 10, 12, 13, 38
Ludington, Henry (father) 4, 6, 7, 8, 9, 10, 12, 13, 14, 16, 18, 22, 24, 26, 38

Ludington, Rebecca (sister) 13, 15
Ludington, Sybil
    birth 12
    children 26, 27
    death 27–28, 30
    marriage 26, 27
Ogden, Edmond (husband) 26, 27
Ogden, Henry (son) 26, 27
Patrick, Louis S. 15, 16
Peck, Julia 27
Prescott, Samuel 21
Prosser, Ichabod 14, 15
Revere, Paul 18, 19–20, 21, 22, 23, 36
Revolutionary War 12, 13, 17, 18, 27, 29, 30, 39
Ross, Betsy 32
Schuyler, Catherine 8
Schuyler, Philip 8
Sons of Liberty 23
Spy: A Tale of the Neutral Ground 17
Sybil: Daughter of the American Revolution 35
Sybil Ludington: The Call to Arms 9, 27
Sybil Ludington: The Female Paul Revere 35
Warren, Joseph 18, 20, 21
Washington, George 9, 19, 22

48